Grateful acknowledgements to the publications where these poems first appeared: *American Mustard* ("Some Notes on Walking"); *Carnival* ("I Was a Dancer Once"); *Crack the Spine* ("Which Moths Break in and Steal?"); *issue.ZERO* ("We Girls Grow Up"); *Rip Rap* ("Salt"); *Spot Literary Magazine* ("Funny—34N, 120W," "Sticky," and "Too Smart"); *Tears in the Fence* ("…and the end of day is aquarium colored").

www.pictureshowpress.net

Cover image: Anna Lugova, istockphoto.com

FIRST EDITION

ISBN-13: 978-1-7324144-0-2
ISBN-10: 1732414408

How quietly the heart breaks, almost soundlessly, or with a sound like a piano being played by some lost love, somewhere in a city that might be Paris, the notes flicked by the wind and falling at a woman's feet like little threats. In these poems, Suzanne Allen imbues grief with a kind of magic, loss with a kind of shadow music all its own. So that we're glad to have been broken, too, because we've also been transformed.

— Cecilia Woloch

Little Threats

Suzanne Allen

Picture Show Press

POEMS

Which Moths Break in and Steal?   11
An Extra Hour   12
Last Train   13
Hand-Me-Downs   15
We Girls Grow Up   16
A Feral Child   17
Sticky   19
Nuit blanche   20
Some Notes on Walking   21
Salt   22
Fuck Saturdays   23
Funny—34N, 120W   24
Sephora   25
Don't, Marie.   26
Napkins   28
Writing Desk   29
I Was a Dancer Once   31
Rings   32
Too Smart   34
Inheritance   39
...and the end of day is aquarium colored   41

Not all of them. That's for sure. Some just flutter about in the
street lamps all night and not all of them are assigned the
complicated task. Most do not have a propensity to carry off with
any more than they can nibble for themselves. But the ones with a
tenacious persistence, the ones that will fly in your face evading
the swing of a hand or magazine, these are the ones who will rob
you blind. Not the silver, not the gold jewelry, not even the
woolen coats and sweaters where the others flock. It's the love
letters they're after, and the photographs. So why not just burn
them all? Watch the real daredevils rush into the flames.

An Extra Hour

The first day after daylight savings ends
is always the most surreal. The sun hangs
too far south suddenly, and all Sunday long

the clocks drag an hour behind it.
Not that I mind. Time is so soluble that,
with this shift of the short hand one hour

into the past, it becomes redundant.
I stayed awake last night to see how it felt
to spend an hour twice—that hour when

it becomes 1AM again. The numbers on my
white-bright desktop flashed back like a gift
from someone who knows me well. Feeling

grateful enough not to waste it, I cleaned
up an old love poem and, just before turning
out the light, finished a fantasy for Nancy

Friday about a Paris cabaret. Now the promise
of early sunset—the extra evening hour lit
with candles, the computer screen answering

in letters—lures me, lends an urgency to this
afternoon. The sun slides, warms places far
away from now. Sky beneath the awning, full.

This girl, she has a weakness for all kinds
of boys. The ones that look like the romantic
hero of *Delicatessen* who saves
the damsel from a flooding bathroom and plays
the saw, the ones that look like Arabian
nights with bright stars in their light
eyes, the American ones that look like home
at first glance, and the ones with accents, broken
English or glasses, certain girls
that swing both ways, the ones
who've found their sea legs.

She comes home late and not quite drunk,
alone, to a love that can't contain her,
could never tame her
and wonders why
all her crushes fall away, why she insists
on this catch and release, the chase. She'd stay
'til two or three if there weren't this incessant *souci*
of the *dernier train*, 'til morning if not
for her old-shoe love at home.

Someone she spoke with earlier this evening told her
her French was very good, her mispronunciations—
very charming. She wants to record every word
that she hears—the fights of lovers in late-night
stations, lost and lashing out at each other,
forked tongues and eyes wet
with longing and regret. Nothing.

She regrets nothing but laments every almost love
she's ever had, keeps her wrong-way

tickets as signs but knows there is rarely, if
ever, time to go back. Some
moments just pass like trains, fast, past a platform
where everyone's looking away as if it didn't matter
that they all want to go the same place.

The silver box of her trinkets is heart shaped
and felt lined—a gift from me which has now
found itself back in my possession, badly tarnished.

It wasn't expensive, but I won't donate it. Not
yet. It holds a blue-faced watch that always
matched the suits she wore to work. I can still

see it on our coffee table with so much clutter,
unclasped, her wrist freed to smoke, to lift
margaritas to her thirsty lips. Now it ticks

but no longer keeps time. She spent so much of it,
time, watching televangelists—these lapel pins,
rewards for her faith and frequent donations.

The night she died she wrote a prayer on a page
in her journal, "Lord, deliver me from this pain."
And He did. He could have sent her a sense

of purpose instead of all these pins, unless
she never asked for that. Maybe she was happy.
I wrap the watch around my bedside lamp, put

the pins in the wastebasket. Find the handle
of a silver spoon bent into a ring. The patina
is her mother's. I never saw her wear it—

flowers and scrolls embossed in the precious
metal. She must have sometimes tried it on late
at night just to feel the slant of the broken circle.

We Girls Grow Up

I knew my dad had gone with his records. No more
cereal at the kitchen counter. No more weekends
in the yard, every-other only. I became my mother's

guardian—a tiny control freak holding in her shit
until it hurt—hating her when she wasn't the mother
I wanted. She never judged me, never lectured

her small aching replica who couldn't just let go.
She tried to save me—tell me everything would be
alright. I read her the warnings on her Pall Mall

Golds. She sacrificed, sent men away when I was *not
easy*, gave me chores I wouldn't do until she broke
down begging for help. A child, I didn't know how

hard it was to ask. So this is how we girls grow up
one day—while daddies look the other way—one
hand on the hot water, the other wiping the soap

from our eyes, half drowning in memories of mothers
drinking and praying—needing—we learn to love
to feel the grown-up holes that one good fuck can't fill.

I was born the Thursday before Memorial Day.
This was no accident. Dr. Varga induced labor
so that it wouldn't interrupt his weekend golf trip.
I always remember that blood-soaked hour as
having been earlier than it actually was, but at least
the weather was mild and I would not be expected
to walk for nearly a year. After all, we had not yet
walked on the moon, and a thirteen year-old named Genie
had spent the last twelve years locked in a bedroom
in a nearby town, strapped to a potty chair, staring
at a yellow raincoat. When discovered—as if
such a girl can, in fact, be discovered—she was all
bunny-walk and sniff, spit and claw. Meanwhile,

I ate well and my mother feared for my figure.
She made me clothes to match her own, and
her brother wrote once from Vietnam—*too bad
it's not a boy!* Nixon promised to bring him home
by Christmas after lowering the legal voting age
to 18, but Genie would never be able to vote
and she would be abused for years by foster parents
and researchers. Even I was once harassed
by a dark-haired man in a silver car with red seats.
He was wearing tighty whities and looking
for his wiener dog—*Do you know what a wiener
dog looks like?* he asked me, and I ran. At about
that same time, Genie retreated into irreversible

silence, refused to open her mouth. "Latch-key kids"
is what they called us when our parents divorced
and our moms had to work and there was only
cold spaghetti to come home to in the afternoon.

She drove a paneled Pinto with jingling hubcaps
and an A.M. radio, sewed small bells into
my petticoats. I wanted to slip into that purple
bottle with Barbara Eden, blink my eyes and
give myself to vapor and sulk, sit cross-legged
in billowing, pink harem pants and wait—
for my dad to come in his shiny new Porsche and
drive me away from the other kids whose fathers
never came, the shy boy around the corner who didn't
have anything to say.

Waiting for his call, I thin
my nail polish. Prince George's
Passion has thickened
since last winter. Instead, I put
Cosmopolitan on my toes—
chocolate with an opalescent flash.

While it dries, I unscrew the other
brushes—one shaped
like a cone atop a glass scoop
of Mauve Ice—wipe the threads
of the tiny jars with remover,
drop the spent cotton into the clean,
white bowl where it floats,
then sinks—Raisin Rage
looking strange as first blood.   Find
the bold red of an old friend—I'm Not
Really a Waitress—in the bottom
of a bathroom drawer. I drip
thinner into the vials,
screw on the tops, then shake.
The silver balls click and stir
memories from that summer—
my same Native Berry quick-dry
on Grandma's abandoned vanity.

Pistol Packin' Pink shimmers—
cotton candy in first-date moonlight—
recalls an aunt's gesticulations.
Lavender Lace Sheer—pearly white,
the shade my mother wore while waiting
for his call—all the rage in 1978.

Nuit blanche

Making line breaks was never as it is here,
now, with you, and there is no one
I can tell, few who would
understand why I insist, twist my hair,
close my eyes when you're near, touch
your face, your piercings. If permission
is a double-edged sword, then let's cut
to the part where you kiss me
again. Pleasure scars
in all directions—loves lost,
lives left
behind, all the wanted
things and people gleaming
sharply at light's vanishing point.

The Camel tins are stacked, our ashes
strewn. No one more inopportune.
Our ghosts line up near the candle,
cast slant nets of shimmer across the table
and I count the dead roses hanging
from your high ceiling. Still, I want this
sleepless night, this
dim corner of your small room, longer
than last year, until all the birds
have come and gone, come and gone
a thousand times. In the morning
you lean languid in your door frame
as I leave, sunlight
spilling in behind you, your slim
shadow sprawled across the landing. *Envie.*
What I want,
it never, ever sleeps.

Two A.M., rain-slicked rue—
you know the one.
He asks me to define
the word and I stop, say
I can't, at first, because
actually it's that Indian restaurant
where you and I have shared
so many courses and words, where
we always ask for a refill
on the spiciest sauce. It is
the spiciest sauce, and it is
all those words, but I can't
say that to *him*, about *you*, about
us, so I stammer, shift my weight
from leg to leg. Such heavy
thoughts so late at night.
I say it lasts, and that it is
a transitive verb,
knowing you can only hurt
an object. It is itself
an object, a common noun
pursued sometimes with such
fervor that it's rendered
priceless, but you can do it
to money and freedom.
You can even do it to your gilded
cage. It is the line I traced
down his back with my tongue
almost as soon as I wanted to. Even then
it was that, and I knew it,
and I said it, too.

Salt

It's just me and him
talking, waiting for water
to boil—the beginnings of bubbles,
a stainless
steel sea. And then
he pours the salt. White
clouds rise then burst to the surface,
hissing. Then nothing.

We pretend we didn't mean it,
sip our wine, stir.
I ask if he could have been more
patient, added it slowly, a few grains
at a time.
Whatever, he says.
It's boiling now. Let's cook.

I forget
he never says he's sorry, let him
season me there on the butcher block
until the smoke alarm reminds us—salt
burning on the stove.

We sleep well, then we sleep some more.
My waking is, nonetheless, ugly. We wait
for her to call, argue about what to do,
what's been done.

He explains his lack of love logically,
describes how he has divided himself. Tall
pink rose buds drop their heads
in the morning sun, never opened. The dog
complains and pulls at the end
of his leash. We lean toward the door.

He explains some more. His many parts.
(Don't piss him off.) Cynicism sets in,
a pool of fresh air, water that I dive into,
a retreat from too much light and noise,
not white.

Maybe red like the dark hall that we follow
to the elevator, where the mirror says
I look tired. There are too many people
on the streets. Fuck Saturdays.

Funny—34N, 120W

I step outside—
        breathe midnight-blue,
                taste the stars.
Laughter stumbles
        through the mini blinds and out
                the open windows,
echoes in the palms across the street
too. Make me believe—
                I am not alone.

Inside, the fire
        cackles—talk of ski clothes
                and careers
        flies about the tea-lit room.
The screen door slams on the
not-so-Christmas night
        behind four smokers,
                the drunkest girl.

Like that time
        on the Air Bus—dark sky
                above and below us,
Tom & Jerry in front
        in headrest TVs
—flying away in recirculated air
laughing
                hysterically,
annoying the woman in seat 20D.

Out of makeup, I pass through
the sliding doors, find
the familiar display—basic
black, face parts illuminated,
detached. Twenty-two euros.

Hopeful, I hand my carte bleue
to the clerk. If it doesn't work
I don't have to wear makeup
tomorrow. Risk
rejection. Do it for the poem.
The dog. Yourself. You
deserve it, this makeup. You
need it.

She thanks me
with samples of wrinkle cream.

Don't, Marie.

Black-eyed and necklaced in gold
she almost smiles, thinks
she might jump from the Pont
Marie or slowly descend
the stone steps to the water slapping
the quai... Don't, Marie.

He only did it once. Now
she carries him on her shoulders—
the weight of the world—one
of his hands blocks her depth perception.
How far *is* the water? Upstairs,
inside, he drinks and toasts the purple
phantoms of his youth.

Remember, she thinks,
when our toes touched the clouds?
How it felt to sweep skyward, then
be pulled back to the tracks in the sand,
tracks without trains or veins or any other things
to carry her blood and bones away
besides the tide.

But green is the color of healing and
things left in the shade too long, so she waits—
for rain and thunder, a crack of light in the sky
bluer than she, strains her white
eyes but can't see
the colors, only the banister up there

in their window... His piano notes
sliding down, and all around her the wind

flicks them at her feet like little threats,
like rain. Somewhere in a room up there
she once slept, soundly—the sheets on the day,
bed the color of memory, of dreams—

but the railing can't save them—these
notes, those dreams—couldn't
be any less useful. She can't see the colors,
only the black-eyed notes
tumbling, light split by the panes.
Splitting pain.

Something she meant to say before
she shut the door.

Napkins

Have you ever counted your lovers—
forgetting some, remembering too few?
You write their names in order
on napkins you can throw away and
swear there were more of them.
You wonder—
Do the missing ones still count?

You remember a place
but forget if you actually slept,
or you remember a face or forearms—
how they talked you into things. But the names—

where are they? How many
kisses forgotten since the last napkin?

It takes a while
to move into inherited
furniture—
maybe weeks
to fill old drawers,
a few months to fasten
on the new hardware she
chose which I
had intended to replace.

She sanded off nearly all
the ivory paint,
put on her makeup here.
There are rings of blush
and other shades of
cosmetic dust
in the naked finish.

I decide not to rush into
repainting.

Soon enough her vanity
makes an unintentional
bedside table—not too low
with books stacked to raise
the alarm clock.
The shelf underneath
holds crochet work
and hand-made draperies
of three generations,
a piggy bank fattened
for April in Paris. Her faux

glass knobs really are
too gaudy, but what works
is the pink wood showing.

But weren't we all?
I am grateful now,
teetering on my right
leg beside the canal—
no, no teeter at all—
balanced, twisting my left
leg in the air, unwinding
the dog's leash. This
happens to us often,
this entanglement, this
dance, though usually,
I fall down all on my own.
An ankle turned on a crack
or cobblestone, knee
skinned, camera crushed.
Amazing how this one
keeps working. Not
a graceful picture.

But dance we must and
remember we might.
Pictures help, and words.
In time, images turn
on themselves, blur
like these upside-down
buildings, gables on green
water, a duck and her
V-shaped wake. No.
Growing older is no
Swan Lake.

Rings

If you try on rings in winter,
remember:
The cold has had its effects—
and the wind—on your hands.
They are slightly smaller.
Perhaps chaffed, more
wrinkled like they will be
in a few more years.
They will look like your
mother's, your grandmothers'.
Do not be alarmed.
Buy the rings. They
would have. Wear them
even on days when you don't
wear makeup.

Of course, these aren't diamonds
or any gemstone. You have those,
have had those and lost them.
Learned the impermanence of things
and people, suspected
lovers and housekeepers
of pawning your family jewels,
imagined them
on someone else's hand.
The ones you used to take
from your grandmothers' drawers.
Ring boxes—tiny thrones buried
in dumps. Giant rubies, an alexandrite.
Her pajama-time "skin-the-bunny"
gone, lifted from your
life like so many

T-shirts and turtlenecks. Tug

on the ring. If it is hard
to take off, then good.
A cheap ring will adjust
for summer swell, but remember:
The beach is no place for rings.
Aquamarine, pink tourmaline
are lovely in spring.

Too Smart

My sister told me once that I was too smart for my own good.
    "That's what your problem is."
    She said it with discovery in her voice.
Now, I've spent most of my life trying to *get* smart, *be* smart,
    and it never occurred to me that I could be *too* smart.
    I have, however, learned that—contrary to popular
    American opinion—you *can* be too rich, and too thin.
    I know from watching.
There's a different kind of knowing, like how
    We know there are pretty sisters, and then there are
    the smart ones. I haven't yet figured out why
    it is this way. I just know.
I also know my sister doesn't know she's pretty.
    And she certainly doesn't think she's
    smart. I'm the smart one, remember.
She brought me a dozen long stemmed roses from the Farmers'
    Market. She knows I love both pink and white roses.
    Pretty and thoughtful… Giant
    white heads with plush pink tips on their center petals, and
    long, straight stems. In two days the roses will be
    potpourri.
But today they are amazing.
They stand a bit awkwardly in the clear glass vase
    with their long stems, but I can't bring myself
    to cut them. They would arrange better if I could—
    like when I finally cut my hair. It was too long too.
So I'll go ahead and cut the roses.

Much better. Was I hesitant to cut the long
    stems because they gave the roses value?
I don't know why I waited so long to cut my hair—
    because it felt like the one thing that made me pretty?

My grandma taught me to love roses—despite their thorns,
    See's Candy, and pretty things like tea cups,
    and shoes, and a lovely wine glass. She loved me.
I know this. She also begrudged me. "Oh, you think
    you're so smart." She would look at me like
    something villaine—like a woman who would steal
    away with her husband.
    My grandma was suspicious of women. Of course,
    when I was a girl, I usually *had* gotten away
    with *something* because, well—she spoiled me.
    And she, too, probably said the words "too smart"
    to me a time or two.
I just never thought to question them then.
She died last summer, just days after her ninetieth birthday.
    June is hot as Hell in Havasu, but she
    was always cold. A Cancer to my Gemini,
    she could worry—about the electric outlets, the locks
    on the doors, the burners on the stove and
    the cracks in the pavement.
I worry now too. I worry that I am too smart for my own
    good. And that doesn't sound good.

       *   *   *

They say the more You learn, the less You know.
    The reverse could also be true: The more
    You know, the less You learn. This, for Some,
    I know is true.
Meanwhile, along the way, and repeatedly,
    it has been proven to me—personally, that We
    learn from Our mistakes. Must One learn from One's
    mistakes? And mustn't One first think
    She knows something in order to make a mistake?
    And wouldn't it then stand to reason that the more
    She knew, the more mistakes She would make—
    and so the more still She would learn?

A truth—as We get older, We discover how little
          We actually *can* know.
                    I want a new pronoun—We need a new 'One.'
"One" is too formal. "We" is too assumptive—
          assuming that We have anything, something
          in common. And She slash He, Him slash Her
          just won't do. Neither will His slash Hers.
That's all separate but equal.
And They and Their are plural while I am not.

This is my problem.

I think too much. But don't you agree? We do need
          a new 'one.' All that is Otherness—"woman
          as Other," poet as Other, man as Other. Hmmm…
          wait-a-minute. I like the sound of that one:
          "'…by virtue of a certain lack of qualities'" men, too,
          can achieve Otherness.
Woolf would have said that Charlotte Brontë's work
          suffered under her anger at her
                              Otherness
          …had she not come before Simone de Beauvoir.
No wonder I can't get a date.

Anger isn't pretty. Angry is not   [equal to]
          pretty—my sister isn't angry. Angry is not
          attractive.
I remember my ex-stepmother's angry face. She is
          my sister's mother—
                    Aside—a contemporary family riddle: My
                    sister is my half sister, one of two,
                    and my father has since remarried.
          My ex-stepmother's angry face wasn't beautiful like
          her Other one, the one my father left my mother for—
          the one that made *me* want to leave my mother too.

I was angry at my mother for my father's leaving—for
        a long time, but We didn't call it anger then.
        And by the time I could, it didn't matter anymore.
But I am angry. Today, it is because somewhere,
        a rapist's accuser is bleeding: "Third time in rehab
        since the incident. Her credibility is lost. What
        a surprising turn." We is too ready to dispose of Her.
        No One wants to see that His pattern of using
        Them as objects has created Her lack of credibility.
        Tell me, why does We
        blame Her for her present, but We does not
                                        think
        to hold Him accountable for His past?
I do not think this is too smart of Us.

        *   *   *

Usually, I'm most angry when no One else wants to be.
        And this, I suspect, is what makes me too smart
        for my own good.

I have a rubber Daphne in my medicine cabinet. She just
        showed up in my Christmas stocking
        one year with the socks, and the sea salt, and the
        Chanukah coins. I think my sister put her there.
        She knows I loved Scooby Doo way before
        Nickelodeon since,
        on the rare occasion that I could watch a cartoon
        without my Christian mother riding me, it was
        always Scooby Doo, and
        surprise! It was usually at Grandma's house.
Daphne, Thelma, a jock, a stoner, and Scooby.
        They were mystery solvers who drove around
        in the Mystery Machine—a big green van.
        Thelma wore glasses. I often wish I wore glasses.
        Smart is hot on some chicks, but not

on poor Thelma. At the least opportune moments,
Thelma would trip or slip and fall and lose her
glasses, and her way. Daphne was feminine
and slender with big, bouncing orange hair—
                              long hair.
Daphne of my medicine cabinet is about four inches tall.
    Her pale rubber legs are bendable, but mostly
    she stands erect next to the toothpaste, her arms
    outstretched with two large hands
    protruding from her groovy, purple sleeves. One
    hand is pointed like a gun, both palms face up. They
    aren't quite the same color as her legs, these
    big hands. They're sort of grey.
Still, Daphne was the pretty one. Thelma was the smart one.
    Only, they weren't sisters. I can't even say
    they were friends.

Do you think too—as I do—that Thelma knew about *too*
    smart? Anyway, she always cracked the case.

Starting at the back, she flips the atlas
pages, left thumb loosing several silver
edges at a time. She watches, vacant,
as continents fly by, and on the roof,
the sound of nothing—muffled like the tantrum
a grown-up child screams into a pillow.

Her mother made this one, the faded pillow
on her lap that props up the atlas.
It matched the faded sofa, evoked tantrums
from her sisters like the family silver did.
The Christmas lights still strung around the roof
cast their colors on the weedy, vacant

lot next door, fall steady on the vacant
floor. She sits against the wall, the pillow
on her lap, this room beneath the roof
sprawled out and empty as Antarctica,
while at her sister's, freshly polished silver
sleeps in velvet drawers. Though temper tantrums

never were her gift, she thinks a tantrum's
maybe what she needs to snap this vacant
feeling loss unfurls—a rushing, silver
Nile—loss as lush as Mother's pillow
winds for miles, four thousand says the atlas.
More in rainy seasons. This old roof

has lived no more, no less than other roofs.
It's seen divorce and death, too many tantrums
to count. But when she opens wide the atlas,
finds the green and beige and blues so vacant,

she wants to stop her breath inside this pillow.
A draft creeps in and makes her shiver silver.

She breaks the atlas binding. Shining silver
frosts her vacant days under this roof—
throwing tantrums for no one, fluffing pillows.

— Colette's "Le miroir"

Fortunately, breathing under water
is easier, now that I admit to the drowning.

Even in this blue-green half-light, the cancer
stinks up the room—floats—covered in the white
sheets of nostalgia. The quiet is blinding.

Someone's nephew is someplace else now, and we
are here remembering—fast cars from another world,

racing. The quiet is not as blinding as it is heavy,
heavy as a Hemi at the bottom of a
fish tank. The old blowfish is alive and well,

just not here, in this restaurant, in this desert
where fish are a tourist attraction. The brothers

will argue over who gets to pay the bill and be
thankful to be able. They like the blowfish story.
Don't talk about the liver, the poisonous ovaries,

the sleeping pills of denial. Such tales keep me
up at night. All this sand is just tumbled rocks

slowly releasing their fossils into the currents.
Motor homes whir out of town, comforting
their passengers with the promise of blue-green

landscapes, but there cannot be enough water,
not anywhere in the world, to console this caravan.

*In this short story, an older, and presumably wiser Colette has a
conversation with her fictional double, Claudine, about youth and aging.*

Born and raised in the San Gabriel Valley of Southern California, Suzanne Allen teaches writing. She has an MFA in Poetry from California State University, Long Beach, and she is a Pushcart Prize nominee with poems published in journals and anthologies around the world, such as *Cider Press Review, Pearl, Nerve Cowboy, Hobo Camp Review, Not a Muse: the Inner Lives of Women, a World Poetry Anthology* (Haven Books); *Veils, Halos & Shackles*, (Kasva Press); *Villanelles*, (Everyman's Library Pocket Poet Series.) She is a co-editor of *The Bastille: the Literary Magazine of Spoken Word Paris*, and the founder of Small Fish Big Pond. Her first chapbook, *verisimilitude*, is available from Corrupt Press. She lives in Long Beach with her Shih Tzu, Filou.

www.ingramcontent.com/pod-product-compliance
Lightning Source LLC
Chambersburg PA
CBHW021147020426
42331CB00005B/943